Piano/Vocal Selections

SIDE SHOW

Book and Lyrics by Bill Russell
Music by Henry Krieger

D1517177

Music edited by David Chase

Interior show photos by Joan Marcus

ISBN 0-7935-9162-7

HAL•LEONARD®
CORPORATION
7777 W. BLUEMOUND RD. P.O. BOX 13819 MILWAUKEE, WI 53213

Visit Hal Leonard Online at
www.halleonard.com

The Hilton Sisters introduce themselves to Buddy, Terry and the audience in "When I'm By Your Side."

SIDE SHOW

CONTENTS

Terry and Buddy visit the Hilton Sisters before their debut.

The Boss of the Side Show offers Terry and Buddy a private viewing of the Hilton Sisters.

"We Share Everything" a production number in the first act.

The Hilton Sisters in the Egyptian extravaganza "We Share Everything."

"Come Look at the Freaks."

Jake confesses his love for Violet in "You Should Be Loved."

SYNOPSIS

Side Show was inspired by the lives of Daisy and Violet Hilton, conjoined twins born in Brighton, England in 1908. While still children, they moved to America and became known as "San Antonio's Siamese Twins." The Hilton Sisters became star attractions on the vaudeville circuit, earning over $3,000 a week during the Great Depression. In 1936, Violet was married on the fifty-yard-line of the Cotton Bowl in front of a paying audience as the finale of the Texas Centennial celebration. On film they appeared in Tod Browning's *Freaks* and a '50s B-film called *Chained for Life*. Daisy and Violet died of influenza within hours of each other in North Carolina in 1969.

Side Show begins with the Company seated on bleachers, staring at the audience. The Boss rises and exhorts customers to see his attractions -- including the Bearded Lady, the Reptile Man, the Bride of Snakes and to hear the "haunting song of the Siamese Twins" ("Come Look at the Freaks").

Buddy Foster, a young musician with aspirations of becoming a song-and-dance man, brings Terry Connor, a talent scout for the Orpheum Circuit to see the Siamese Twins. Buddy contends he could create an act for them. Terry is dubious but, after seeing them, reluctantly agrees to try to meet them.

The Boss offers the two men an opportunity to privately view the "fleshly link" for a "small consideration." The three interrupt a birthday party for the twins, thrown by their sideshow friends ("Happy Birthday to You and to You"). The Boss leaves Jake, an African-American who plays the "Cannibal King" in the sideshow, with the twins and their visitors. Terry stops them from exposing their connection and asks them their names and eventually to tell him their hopes and dreams. Violet wants a husband and home, Daisy wants stardom ("Like Everyone Else").

Terry asks Jake to get the Boss, who is far from happy finding the men still there. Terry offers him a cut of the twins' potential vaudeville earnings. The Boss rudely refuses and orders Jake to show the two off the grounds. Terry and the twins convince Jake to help them, and a plan is hatched. Buddy will teach Violet and Daisy a song which they will perform for their sideshow friends, and if that goes well Terry will book them in vaudeville. After Terry and Buddy leave, Jake asks Daisy and Violet to consider the consequences of possibly leaving their sideshow family and the whole group voices its conflicting opinions ("The Devil You Know").

Two weeks later Terry returns and admits to himself that an uncontrollable attraction to Daisy has brought him back. Buddy tells him the personal situation is getting sticky, that he thinks Violet is sweet on him and Daisy constantly asks about Terry. Terry dismisses these concerns and suggests giving the girls flowers. Backstage before their secret debut performance, Daisy confesses to her sister that she loves Terry and coaxes Violet into admitting she is enamored of Buddy ("Feelings You've Got to Hide").

The Hiltons' secret debut is a smashing success ("When I'm By Your Side"). But the Boss is awakened by the cheers and applause and physically threatens the twins. Jake intervenes and the other attractions threaten to quit. Faced with the loss of his whole enterprise, the Boss has no choice but to let Daisy and Violet leave. The sideshow family bids them a sad farewell ("Say Goodbye to the Freak Show").

Before the twins' vaudeville debut, Terry tries to convince a dubious group of male reporters that the two will be an overnight sensation. Backstage, Daisy blatantly asks Terry for a good show kiss. Violet is embarrassed by her sister's flirting, and an argument ensues ("Leave Me Alone").

On stage, the Hilton Sisters appear as ancient Egyptian Queens discovered in double sarcophagi and then share fancy footwork with some dancing pharaohs ("We Share Everything"). Backstage after the performance, the reporters assault them with questions which become increasingly rude, especially about the twins' love-lives. Terry and Buddy both deny any romantic interest. Left alone, Daisy and Violet wonder if they will ever be loved ("Who Will Love Me As I Am?").

Act II begins with the Hilton Sisters at the height of their success – a lavish Follies number ("Rare Songbirds on Display"). Buddy asks Jake if he knows why Violet seems unhappy, and Jake guesses it's because Daisy has achieved her dream of stardom, but Violet seems no closer to hers of having a husband.

At a fancy New Year's Eve party, Buddy tries clowning with Violet to cheer her up and unexpectedly finds himself asking her to marry him. After some hesitation, she accepts and, in the excitement, suggests a big double wedding. Terry side-steps the possibility and, left by himself, imagines what it would be like if only he could be alone with Daisy. ("Private Conversation").

On stage, the sisters have added Buddy to their act ("One Plus One Equals Three"). But backstage, both Daisy and Buddy separately express doubts as to how the marriage will actually work. Jake overhears Buddy and tries to save Violet from imminent heartbreak by confessing he's always secretly loved her ("You Should Be Loved"). He asks her to marry him instead of Buddy, but Violet longs to be seen as normal and couldn't bear the whispers and stares that would come with loving someone of a different race.

The night before the big wedding at the Texas Centennial, Daisy is feeling neglected. To appease her, Terry suggests the four spend some time alone together by taking a ride through the Tunnel of Love. In the darkness, some unsettling truths become evident. Buddy is so aware of Daisy's presence that he loses all romantic interest in Violet. Daisy and Terry, as alone as they will ever be, let their passions run wild. Violet realizes she is feeling much more heat coming from Daisy's side than from Buddy's ("Tunnel of Love").

The next day in a dressing area inside the Cotton Bowl, Jake announces he's leaving, which greatly unsettles Violet. Terry is furious with Jake, who in turn explodes at Buddy for not telling Violet the truth. Buddy confesses that he loves Violet, "but not the way you want." Tod Browning, a famous movie director, arrives from Hollywood for the wedding and to offer the Hiltons parts in his new film. When Violet announces the wedding is off, Daisy asks Terry to marry her. But Terry can't bring himself to publicly acknowledge the passion he made so evident in the Tunnel of Love. Daisy tells him their relationship is over, both personally and professionally. Left alone, Daisy and Violet find comfort in each other ("I Will Never Leave You").

The wedding proceeds. Daisy and Violet ironically sing "Come Look at the Freaks" with full knowledge and acceptance of who they are.

HENRY KRIEGER

COMPOSER

Born in New York in 1945, Henry Krieger began his musical journey early in life listening to Chopin and Liszt as an infant. As he grew up his tastes expanded to include great R&B artists like Fats Waller, Ray Charles, Jackie Wilson and the Drifters. Basically a self-taught composer, his parents introduced him to Broadway . . . and Henry's award winning musical style was instilled.

A multi-talented individual who had not yet focused on his eventual career, Henry entered the publicity field staying long enough to conduct interviews with many personalities including Woody Allen, Joan Rivers, Rodney Dangerfield and the Lettermen. In his own company, he personally represented Jerry Butler for a time.

Henry began to perform in clubs around New York singing other people's material. However, he was already formulating his own writing skills and creating his own songs as well. While composing for Off-Off-Broadway he met Tom Eyen and together they wrote *The Dirtiest Musical,* adapted from Tom's original hit Off-Broadway play, *The Dirtiest Show in Town.*

Mr. Krieger collaborated once more with Tom Eyen resulting in the Grammy Award (Best Original Cast Album) for his score of the Tony Award (6) winning Broadway Musical, *Dreamgirls*. He also composed the music for another long running hit musical which garnered two Tony Awards, *Tap Dance Kid*.

In addition to his theatre credits, Mr. Krieger has written and composed shows which have been produced internationally as well as throughout the United States.

He wrote both music and lyrics to *Fat Pig,* which sees life and death through the eyes of farm animals. The show enjoyed a highly successful run at Britain's Leicester Haymarket Theatre in 1988, appealing to the old and young alike and achieving critical acclaim.

Henry composed the musical score for *Dangerous Music,* written with his *Dreamgirls* collaborator, Tom Eyen, produced at the Burt Reynolds Jupiter Theatre. The show enjoyed wide critical acclaim and enthusiastic audience reception.

Television credits include numerous Miss America Pageant telecasts as well as the inclusion of Henry's songs in a variety of programs around the world. He has also written extensively for children's television including three seasons for the legendary Captain Kangaroo. Henry serves as musical director for the 52nd Street Project, a much hailed theatrical outreach program for children from the Clinton (Hell's Kitchen) area of New York City.

Most recently, Mr. Krieger has composed songs and musical scenes for the Radio City Music Hall's world famous *Christmas Spectacular*. He has also written *Love's Fowl*, a revolutionary one-act puppet opera written with Susan J. Vittucci.

Side Show sang through Henry's heart early on and is an undertaking he will always cherish. This musical, for which the critics raved, received four Tony nominations ... one being for the Best Score!

Mr. Krieger is a creative soul always seeking out new projects that lift the spirit.

BILL RUSSELL

LIBRETTIST

Bill Russell was born and raised in the Black Hills of South Dakota. His paternal grandparents were Wyoming ranchers, and his father was known as "Cowboy" to everyone. But foregoing his Wild West background, Bill was bitten by a theater bug at an early age.

He attended Morningside College in Sioux City, Iowa, for two years, majoring in theater and spent the summers directing shows at a resort in northern New Jersey. There he met an Oberlin student, Janet Hood, and, inspired by *Hair*, convinced her they should write a rock musical together. They did — entirely by mail — and the result was presented at the University of Kansas, where Bill transferred his education. That show, a modern version of the Icarus myth titled *Sun, Son*, won the BMI Inter-Varsity Show Competition for original musicals.

Continuing to write with Ms. Hood, Bill took a detour from musical theater into pop music. With Linda Langford, Janet formed a duo called Jade & Sarsaparilla, and Bill managed them and wrote their lyrics. They toured successfully in New England for several years in the mid-1970s, released an album on Submaureen Records, and made television appearances both locally and nationally.

In 1980, Bill made his Off-Broadway debut, penning book and lyrics for *Fourtune* (music by Ronald Melrose). The show ran for over half a year at the Actors Playhouse and was subsequently performed around the country and in Rio de Janeiro. In 1985, he teamed up with composer Albert Evans and co-author and lyricist Frank Kelly to create *The Texas Chainsaw Musical* Off-Broadway — a revue of unlikely musicals.

In 1987, *Family Style*, with music by Janet Hood, was presented by the Minnesota Musical Theater Workshop, and in 1989 their AIDS piece titled *Elegies for Angels, Punks and Raging Queens* premiered Off-Off-Broadway, with Bill directing. Subsequently, he directed other productions around the country and three in London, including the West End production at the Criterion. *Elegies...* has been produced in Germany, Israel and Australia, among many other countries.

In 1991, *Pageant*, another collaboration with Evans and Kelly, opened Off-Broadway at The Blue Angel where it ran for over a year. That project was directed by Robert Longbottom and subsequently was produced around America and toured Japan.

Side Show was developed with Henry Krieger and Robert Longbottom over a five-year period. During that time Bill and Henry wrote two songs for the Radio City Music Hall *Christmas Spectacular*, including the opening number "Santa's Gonna Rock and Roll." That production was directed and choreographed by Mr. Longbottom. Krieger and Russell were also commissioned to write "Take the Flame" for the opening and closing ceremonies of Gay Games IV.

Bill greatly looks forward to future projects with his *Side Show* collaborator Henry Krieger and writing many more songs with him.

EMANUEL AZENBERG, JOSEPH NEDERLANDER, HERSCHEL WAXMAN
JANICE McKENNA, SCOTT NEDERLANDER

PRESENT

SIDE SHOW

BOOK AND LYRICS BY
BILL RUSSELL

MUSIC BY
HENRY KRIEGER

WITH

**ALICE
RIPLEY**

**EMILY
SKINNER**

**JEFF
McCARTHY**

**HUGH
PANARO**

**NORM
LEWIS**

**KEN
JENNINGS**

JOHN PAUL ALMON, KRISTEN BEHRENDT, KELLY COLE, BARRY FINKEL, JOHN FRENZER, ANDY GALE, BILLY HARTUNG,
EMILY HSU, TODD HUNTER, ALICIA IRVING, DEVANAND N. JANKI, LAUREN KENNEDY, JUDY MALLOY, DAVID MASENHEIMER,
DAVID McDONALD, MICHELLE MILLERICK, PHILLIP OFFICER, VERNA PIERCE, JIM T. RUTTMAN, J. ROBERT SPENCER,
JENNY-LYNN SUCKLING, SUSAN TAYLOR, TIMOTHY WARMEN, DARLENE WILSON

SCENIC DESIGN BY
ROBIN WAGNER

COSTUME DESIGN BY
GREGG BARNES

LIGHTING DESIGN BY
BRIAN MacDEVITT

SOUND DESIGN BY
TOM CLARK

ORCHESTRATIONS BY
HAROLD WHEELER

CASTING
**JOHNSON-LIFF
ASSOCIATES**

PRESS REPRESENTATIVE
**BILL EVANS
& ASSOCIATES**

MUSICAL COORDINATOR
**SEYMOUR RED
PRESS**

ASSOCIATE CHOREOGRAPHER
**TOM
KOSIS**

GENERAL MANAGER
**ABBIE M.
STRASSLER**

ASSOCIATE PRODUCER
**GINGER
MONTEL**

TECHNICAL SUPERVISOR
**NEIL A. MAZZELLA
BRIAN LYNCH**

PRODUCTION STAGE MANAGER
**PERRY
CLINE**

MUSIC DIRECTION,
VOCAL AND DANCE ARRANGEMENTS
DAVID CHASE

DIRECTED AND CHOREOGRAPHED BY
ROBERT LONGBOTTOM

SIDE SHOW opened at the Richard Rodgers Theatre on October 16, 1997.

Come Look at the Freaks

Words by BILL RUSSELL
Music by HENRY KRIEGER

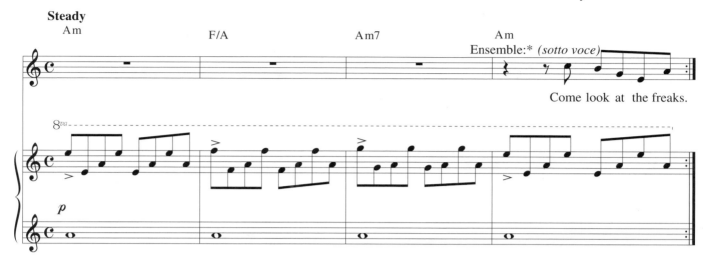

Come look at the freaks.

Come gape at the geeks.

Come ex-a-mine these a- ber - ra - tions, their mal- for-ma-tions, gro- tesque phy-siques.

*Women sing an octave lower.

man turned in - to a rep - tile   As pun-ish-ment for his__ sins.__

Come hear the haunt-ing song__ of the Si - a - mese Twins!__

Come see__ our el - e- gant geek, Re - fined but dead - ly.__ Chick-en

Happy Birthday to You and to You

Words by BILL RUSSELL
Music by HENRY KRIEGER

Like Everyone Else

Words by BILL RUSSELL
Music by HENRY KRIEGER

The Devil You Know

Words by BILL RUSSELL
Music by HENRY KRIEGER

Feelings You've Got to Hide

Words by BILL RUSSELL
Music by HENRY KRIEGER

When I'm By Your Side

Words by BILL RUSSELL
Music by HENRY KRIEGER

You are my fav-'rite new play - mate. I love the fun you pro-vide.

A song and a laugh____ are bet-ter by half____ When I'm

by your side. Hap-py to be your com-pan - ion.

Say Goodbye to the Freak Show

Words by BILL RUSSELL
Music by HENRY KRIEGER

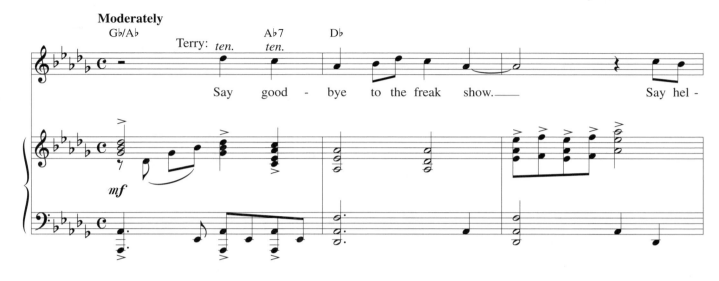

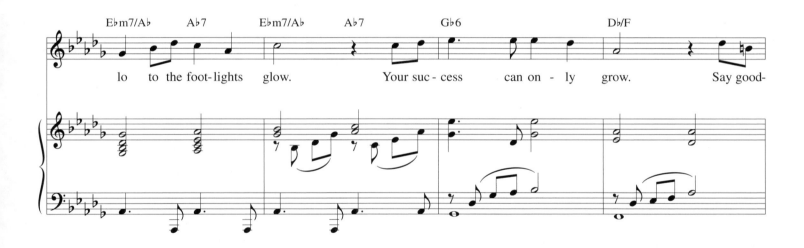

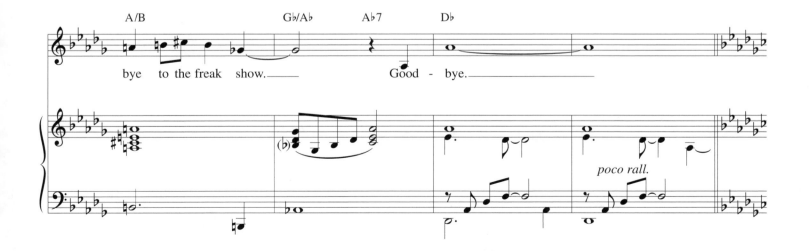

Leave Me Alone

Words by BILL RUSSELL
Music by HENRY KRIEGER

We Share Everything

Words by BILL RUSSELL
Music by HENRY KRIEGER

Who Will Love Me As I Am?

Words by BILL RUSSELL
Music by HENRY KRIEGER

Private Conversation

Words by BILL RUSSELL
Music by HENRY KRIEGER

no - ther,_____ tan - gled and en - twined. I in - vent a sep - a - ra-

- tion in the pri - vate con - ver - sa - tion in my mind._____

_____ I re - solve to say it all._____ Then I hem and haw and

stall._____ For how could I come clean or con - fide?_____ Some - one else_____ is al-

One Plus One Equals Three

Words by BILL RUSSELL
Music by HENRY KRIEGER

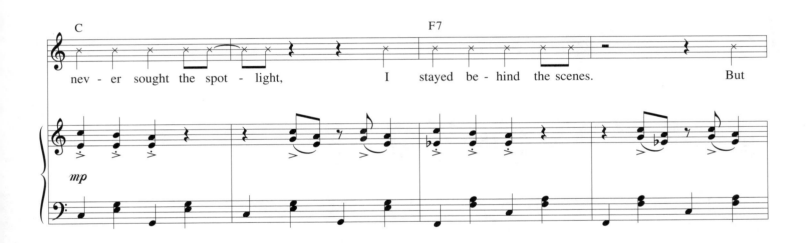

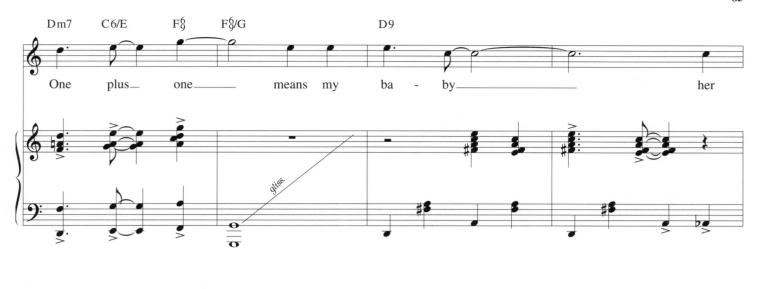

One plus— one ———— means my ba - by———————— her

sis - ter——————— and me!——————————

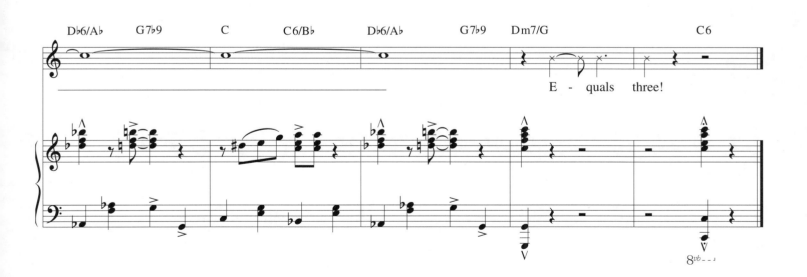

E - quals three!

You Should Be Loved

Words by BILL RUSSELL
Music by HENRY KRIEGER

tries to pro-tect you, al - ways comes through. You should have cho- sen the

one who sup-ports you, al - ways sup- ports you what- ev - er you do. Yes,

you should be loved in the way I love you

Tunnel of Love

Words by BILL RUSSELL
Music by HENRY KRIEGER

Though no one can see___ in the Tun - nel of Love,

there's not a place___ you can hide.___

I Will Never Leave You

Words by BILL RUSSELL
Music by HENRY KRIEGER